The Singer Manufacturing Co., Ltd
Singer, Clydebank.

THE SINGER RECREATION HALL   SINGER

FOREWORD

I N issuing this brochure it is the desire of the Company that the employees may be able to carry to their homes a record, in permanent form, of the devotion displayed by the workers in the Great War. The gallant fighters whose names are here inscribed have fashioned and emblazoned on the scroll of time their own memorials, and yet, while we may not tarnish these by any unworthy endeavour, it is fitting that we should permanently record the names of the employees, who in the seeming hour of the shadow of death proved themselves worthy of the splendid traditions of our manhood.

Facing the main entrance of the Recreation Hall, a Roll of

Honour consisting of three memorial tablets, made in copper and framed in oak, has been placed. On this Roll are inscribed the names of four hundred and eleven employees who made the supreme sacrifice in the hour of our nation's peril.

Within the Hall, and situated on the west wall, are to be found tablets recording the names of two thousand five hundred and eight employees, who also responded to the call of duty and were happily spared.

The Memorial will stand for all time as a record of our pride in the men who put all other considerations aside, and came forward to fight for Empire, Right and Freedom.

Those who were fortunate enough to survive the storm and stress of battle came through with unshaken faith in the cause for which they fought. It is our earnest hope that in raising this Roll of Honour we may at once hearten them to live up to those grand ideals, and, at the same time, leave a tangible reminder to all of the gallant deeds and services which they rendered mankind.

THE SINGER MANUFACTURING CO. LTD.

MAIN ENTRANCE, RECREATION HALL.   SINGER

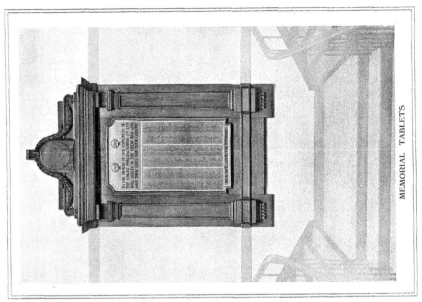

MEMORIAL TABLETS

7

**TO THE MEMORY OF THE
EMPLOYEES OF THE SINGER MANUFACTURING CO., LTD.
WHO SERVED IN THE GREAT WAR AND GAVE THEIR
LIVES FOR THEIR COUNTRY**

Abbot, Robt.
Adams, Charles.
Adams, Charles.
Adams, Robert.
Ahern, Patrick.
Airth, William.
Aitken, David.
Alexander, John.
Allan, John.
Allan, Thomas.
Anderson, George.
Anderson, James.
Anderson, William.
Atkins, J.
Atkinson, James.
Bain, James.
Bain, John.

Baird, Alexander.
Banks, Terrance.
Barclay, Dugald.
Bartlam, William.
Baxter, Robert.
Bennington, George.
Berry, Edward.
Black, Alexander
Black, Daniel.
Black, Daniel.
Blackwood, James.
Blakely, John.
Bolton Samuel.
Boyd John.
Boyle, Arthur.
Brebner, Peter.
Brittain, Archibald.

Brown, Forbes.
Brown, J.
Brown, Thomas.
Bryan, William.
Bryce, Alexander.
Bryce, Charles.
Caldwell, John.
Caldwell, Robert.
Cameron, Malcolm.
Cameron, William.
Campbell, Alexander.
Campbell, Neil.
Campbell, Peter.
Campbell, Thomas.
Carberry, Joseph.
Carr, J.
Carroll, Frank.

Carson, W.
Cattanach, James.
Cavanagh, Gerald.
Charity, James.
Chisholm, William.
Christie, James.
Christie John.
Clague, W.
Cochrane, Alexander.
Cochrane, Andrew.
Collins, George.
Collins, John.
Colquhoun, James.
Conlin, John.
Connelly, John.
Connelly, Joseph.
Convery, Thomas.

Coulter, W.
Cowan, Alexander.
Cowan, Alexander.
Cowden, Alexander.
Cowie, Albert.
Crabb, G
Craigie, Thomas.
Crawford, J.
Crawford, John.
Crichton, Robert.
Cullen, John.
Cunningham, Francis.
Currie, Michael.
Curry, Wm. J.
Cuthbertson, William.
Dakers, G.
Dalrymple, Mungo.
Daly, John.
Daly, Thomas.
Darroch, James.
Davidson, Albert
Davil, William.
Dempsey, James.
Dickson, John.
Docherty, George.
Docherty, John.

Docherty, Patrick.
Doig, J.
Dolan, Robert.
Donaldson, Allan.
Douglas, James.
Downie, George.
Drummond, Alex.
Dunn, Alexander.
Dunn, John.
Dunn, Thomas.
Dunn, Thomas.
Edgar, William.
Elliot, Joseph.
Espy, Alexander.
Evans, Daniel.
Ewart, Alexander.
Ferguson, J.
Ferguson, James.
Ferguson, John.
Ferry, John.
Fitzpatrick, J.
Fitzpatrick, J.
Fleming, William.
Flynn, Thomas.
Fogo, Sam.
Forrest, William.

Fraser, George.
Fraser, James.
Fraser, John.
Fraser, William.
Fraser, William.
Gallagher, James.
Gardner, H.
Gemmell, Archibald.
Gibbons, Joseph.
Gilchrist, Hugh.
Gillan, James.
Gillanders, David.
Gilmour, Edward.
Gilmour, T.
Gilmour, William.
Glendinning, Alex.
Goudie, R.
Gow, William.
Graham, Robert.
Graham, Robert.
Granger, Robert.
Grant, Alexander.
Grant, M.
Gray, Jas. A.
Gray, Robert.
Gray, William.

Green George.
Grieve, William B.
Gunn, D.
Hains, Peter.
Hamilton, Archibald.
Hamilton, David.
Hamilton, William.
Hannah, Ben.
Hannah, George.
Hannah, William
Harris, Peter.
Hart, John.
Hartley, John
Harvie, John.
Haxton, Charles.
Hay, Alexander.
Heggie, Robt. G.
Henderson, James
Henderson, John.
Henderson, William.
Henshilwood, Donald.
Higgins, James.
Hill, Joseph.
Hogg, Rennie.
Holborn John.
Hollister, Charles.

Hunter, Thomas.
Hunter, William.
Irvine, Hugh.
Jack, Robert.
Jack, Thomas.
Jardine, Daniel.
Jardine, Peter.
Jeffrey A.
Johnston, David.
Johnston, Hugh.
Johnston, James.
Johnstone, William.
Joiner, James.
Jordon, Alfred.
Jordon, William.
Keenan, Francis.
Kelly, James.
Kelly, Robert.
Kelpie, John.
Kemp, J.
Kilmartin, Michael.
Kinloch, William.
Kinnear, Andrew.
Kitchen, William.
Knox, George.
Lain, Michael.

Laird, J.
Lamb Wm. M'W.
Latimer, William.
Laughlin, J.
Laverty, John.
Law, Andrew.
Lee, Thomas.
Leitch, Andrew
Leitch, John.
Leitch, Thomas.
Lewis, Norman F.
Lightbody, Daniel
Livingstone, Alex.
Lockhart, A.
Luke, John.
Lynch, James.
M'Adam, R.
M'Arthur, Robert.
M'Ausland, William
M'Callum, William.
M'Cormack, Archd.
M'Crae, Alexander.
M'Crorie, John.
M'Cue, James.
M'Culloch, Robert.
M'Cutcheon, John.

M'Dade, James.
M'Dade, Robert J.
M'Dermid, James.
M'Dougall John.
M'Elwee, John.
M'Fadden, James.
M'Fadden, Matthew.
M'Farlane, Andrew.
M'Farlane, Lachlan.
M'Farlane, William.
M'Geachy, George.
M'Geoff, John.
M'Gill, Charles.
M'Glynn, John.
M'Gregor, John.
M'Guire, David.
M'Guire, Patrick
M'Ilroy, James.
M'Intosh, Andrew.
M'Intosh, Duncan.
M'Intyre, Alex.
M'Intyre, George.
M'Intyre, James.
M'Intyre, James.
M'Intyre, John.
M'Kay, Robert.

M'Kay, Thomas L.
M'Kee, James.
M'Kellar, Archibald.
M'Kellar, George.
M'Kendrick, James
M'Kendrick, James.
M'Kenna, Hugh.
M'Kenzie Robert.
M'Kim, James.
M'Kinlay, John.
M'Kinlay, Robert.
M'Kinnon, Robert.
M'Lachlan, Daniel.
M'Lachlan, George.
M'Lachlan, John.
M'Laren, Alexander
M'Lean, Charles.
M'Lean, J.
M'Lellan, Walter.
M'Leod, James.
M'Leod John.
M'Leod, Murdo.
M'Leod, Sinclair.
M'Luckey, Charles.
M'Luskey, Charles.
M'Mahon, William

10

M'Master, George.	Meechan, George.	Paterson, William.	Ryan, Thomas.
M'Millan, Hugh.	Miller, Findlay.	Patrick, Thomas.	Sadler, Robert W.
M'Millan, James.	Miller, Harry.	Patterson, Alexander.	Sands, Daniel.
M'Millan, James.	Miller, James.	Paul, George.	Scott, J.
M'Murrich, Alexander.	Miller, Robert.	Peel, Robert.	Scott, Robert.
M'Neil, John.	Mitchell, James.	Philip, John.	Scott, William.
M'Neish, James.	Mitchell, Robert.	Philson, Alexander.	Selkirk, John A.
M'Niven, Archibald.	Moir, A.	Philson, John.	Sewell, George.
M'Pherson, Joseph.	Morrison, James.	Philson, John.	Sexton, Michael.
M'Phee, Archibald.	Morrison, Robert.	Phimister, James.	Shaw, D.
M'Rae, Alexander.	Moy, James.	Ponton, James.	Shaw, James.
M'Robert, Alexander.	Murdoch, James.	Proctor, John.	Shaw, James.
M'Swan, Roderick.	Murphy, Thomas.	Purcell, William.	Shaw, John.
M'Taggart, Samuel.	Murray, David.	Queen, John.	Shea, Robert.
M'Whinney, Maxwell.	Murray, Gordon.	Quigley, James.	Sheriff, John.
M'Whirr, Thomas.	Murray, James.	Rae, Alexander.	Shields, Duncan.
Mailer, Andrew.	Naismith, Andrew.	Rafferty, John.	Shields, James.
Maitland, James.	Neave, William.	Ramsay, David.	Sime, William.
Mallany, James D.	Newman, Albert.	Rannochan, James.	Simpson, Duncan.
Malone, John.	Niven, David.	Redpath, Samuel.	Sinclair, Dugald.
Manson, John.	O'Hare, James.	Rennie, Hiram.	Skelton, John.
Marr, Merlyn.	O'Rourke, James.	Richmond, Thomas.	Sleith, William.
Marshal, James.	Orr, William.	Robertson, Donald.	Sloan, Bryce.
Martin, John W.	Paterson, A.	Robertson, James	Smith, A.
Masterton, James.	Paterson, Andrew.	Russel, William.	Smith, James
Meehan, Francis.	Paterson, H.	Russell, William.	Smith, Philip

Snowden, Robert.	Syme, Lawrence.	Torrance, David.	Wilson, Andrew.
Speirs, J.	Tassie, George B.	Turner, Andrew.	Wilson, David.
Speirs, Walter.	Taylor, Harold	Turner, David.	Wilson, Hugh.
Stevenson, Daniel	Taylor, John.	Turner, Francis.	Wilson, Quentin.
Stevenson, John.	Taylor, John.	Walker, Robert.	Wilson, William.
Stevenson, Peter.	Teirney, Joseph.	Walker, Thomas.	Winning, Andrew
Stewart, Joseph.	Temple, Daniel.	Walker, William.	Wood, William.
Stirrat, James.	Temple, Thomas.	Walls, Joseph.	Wright, Edward.
Stoddart, George.	Thompson, William.	Ward, James.	Wylie, John.
Sommerville, Alexander.	Thomson, Alexander.	Watson, Alexander.	Wyllie, George C.
Summers Jeffrey.	Thomson, D.	Wheelan, Christopher.	Yates, Ballantyne.
Swan, John.	Thomson, John.	White, James.	Young, John.
Sweeney, H.	Thomson, Robert.	White, John.	Younger, A.
Sweeney, William.	Thomson, Robert.	Willison, Alexander.	

"*THEIR NAME LIVETH FOR EVERMORE.*"

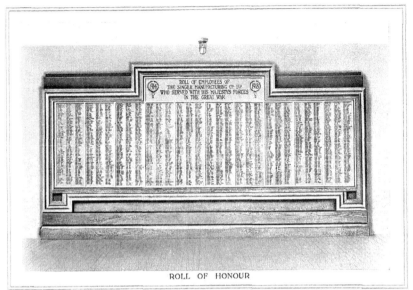

ROLL OF HONOUR

ROLL OF EMPLOYEES OF
THE SINGER MANUFACTURING COMPANY LTD.
WHO SERVED WITH HIS MAJESTY'S FORCES
IN THE GREAT WAR

Abbot, John.
Abercrombie, Neil
Abercrombie, Ralph.
Abernethy, Matthew.
Adam, James.
Adam, John.
Adam, Robert.
Adams, Andrew.
Adams, Duncan.
Adams, William
Adamson, Alexander.
Adamson, John.
Adamson, John.
Agnew, John.
Ahern, John.
Aird, Daniel
Aird, George.

Aird, James.
Aird, John.
Aird, Robert.
Aird, William.
Aitken, Alexander.
Aitken, J.
Aitken, Malcolm.
Aitken, Robert.
Aitken, Thomas.
Aitken, William.
Alexander, Alex.
Alexander, John.
Alexander John.
Alexander, Robert.
Alexander, W.
Allan. Alexander.
Allan, Campbell.

Allan, David.
Allan, George.
Allan, Hugh.
Allan, Robert.
Allan, Robert.
Allan, Thomas.
Allan, William.
Allan, William.
Allan, William.
Allen, J.
Allen, James.
Allison, George.
Alston, Thomas.
Anderson, Alexander.
Anderson, Andrew.
Anderson, Andrew.
Anderson, D.

Anderson, David.
Anderson, George.
Anderson, George.
Anderson, James.
Anderson, Robert.
Anderson, Robert.
Anderson, William.
Andrew, Francis.
Andrew, John.
Andrews, David.
Annesley, Charles.
Arbuckle, Robert.
Archibald, J.
Archibald, John.
Archibald, John.
Armstrong, James.
Armstrong, James.

14

Armstrong, John.	Ball, Edward.	Beggs. William.	Black, Angus.
Armstrong, John.	Ballantyne, James.	Beggs, William.	Black, David.
Armstrong, Matthew.	Balmer, G.	Bell, James.	Black, George.
Armstrong, W.	Balmer, R.	Bell, John.	Black, George.
Arnold, J. K.	Banks, Christopher.	Bell, John.	Black, J.
Arnold, R.	Banks, John.	Bell, John.	Black, James A.
Arthur, James.	Barbour, John.	Bell, John.	Black, John.
Arthur, Thomas.	Barclay, William.	Bell, Thomas.	Black, John.
Atkinson, J.	Barlow, Peter.	Bell, Thomas.	Black, Patrick.
Atkinson, Thomas.	Barnett, Robert.	Bell, Thomas K.	Black, Peter.
Auchencloss, John.	Barr, Dugald.	Bell, William.	Black, Robert.
Auld, James.	Barr, Thomas.	Belshaw, John.	Black, William.
Bagguley, John.	Bathgate, Alexander.	Belshaw, John.	Black, William J.
Bailey, Alexander.	Battison, George.	Belshaw, William.	Blackadder, Charles.
Bailey, J.	Baxter, James.	Bennet, Henry.	Blackburn, John.
Baillie, James.	Baxter, William.	Bennet, James.	Blackburn, Peter.
Baillie, Robert.	Baxter, William.	Bennoch, Archibald.	Blackwood, Aaron.
Bain, John.	Beaton, Alexander.	Benson, James.	Blaikie, William.
Bain, John.	Beaton, Donald.	Berrie, Herbert.	Blain, James.
Bain, Peter.	Beaton, William.	Bethune, Robert.	Blake, James.
Bain, Tom.	Beattie, Christopher.	Betty, William.	Blakely, David.
Baird, John.	Beattie, David.	Beveridge, William.	Bleakley, Charles.
Baker, Thomas.	Beattie, W.	Binnie, John.	Bloomer, Hugh.
Bald, Charles.	Beattie, William.	Birkby, Andrew.	Blyth, Robert.
Bald, Joseph	Beggs, Charles.	Birkens, William.	Boag, William.
Balfour, John.	Beggs, John.	Bisset, Robert.	Bolton, Matthew.

Bolton, Robert.	Breen, Charles.	Brown, T.	Bulloch, Alexander.
Bolton, William.	Bremner, John.	Brown, Thomas.	Bulloch, Robert.
Bonnar, P.	Brennan, Robert.	Brown, Thomas.	Bunnton, William.
Borland, James.	Brennan, T.	Brown, Thomas.	Burgess, Alexander.
Borthwick, James.	Brisbane, Thomas.	Brown, William.	Burgess, Hugh M'F.
Bowie, Alexander.	Brodie, Alexander.	Brown, William.	Burke, Edward.
Bowie, George.	Brodie, James.	Brown, William P.	Burnett, David.
Bowie, T.	Brodie, Thomas.	Brownlie, Alexander.	Burnett, James.
Bowie, William.	Broom, Richard.	Brownlie, Archibald.	Burnett, Matthew.
Bowman, Robert.	Brotherhood, Thomas	Brownlie, Robert.	Burns, F.
Boyd, James.	Brown, A.	Bruce, Alexander.	Burns, James.
Boyd, Robert.	Brown, Allan.	Bruce, Daniel.	Burns, Peter.
Boyd, Thomas.	Brown, Archibald.	Bruce, George.	Burns, Robert.
Boyd, Walter.	Brown, Alexander.	Bruce, George.	Burns, Thomas.
Boyd, Walter.	Brown, D.	Bryan, Thomas.	Burns, William.
Boyle, John.	Brown, David C.	Bryce, John.	Burnside, Alexander.
Boyle, John B.	Brown, George.	Bryce, Robert.	Burr, James.
Boyle, William.	Brown, J.	Bryle, J.	Burrell, Henry.
Boyles, John.	Brown, J.	Bryson, Alexander.	Burrows, Archibald.
Brackenridge, J.	Brown, James.	Buchanan, Archibald.	Butchart, Edwin.
Bradley, Charles.	Brown, John.	Buchanan, D.	Butler, William.
Brady, Edward.	Brown, John.	Buchanan, Edwin.	Byars, David.
Brady, Thomas.	Brown, John.	Buchanan, James.	Byars, James.
Brae, Daniel.	Brown, John.	Buchanan, John.	Cairney, George.
Brannigan, Charles.	Brown, Joseph.	Buchanan, Walter.	Cairns, D.
Brebner, G.	Brown, Matthew.	Buchanan, William.	Cairns, James.

Cairns, John.
Calder, Alexander.
Calder, J.
Calder, Peter.
Caldwell, David.
Caldwell, Hugh.
Caldwell, John.
Caldwell, Robert.
Caldwell, Robert.
Caldwell, William.
Callaghan, Alexander.
Callaghan, James.
Callaghan, James.
Callander, James.
Callender, Charles.
Cameron, Alexander.
Cameron, Alexander.
Cameron, A. J.
Cameron, D.
Cameron, Donald.
Cameron, George.
Cameron, James.
Cameron, John.
Cameron, John.
Cameron, John E.
Cameron, John R.

Cameron, Murdoch.
Cameron, Peter.
Cameron, Peter.
Cameron, Robert I.
Cameron, Thomas.
Cameron, William.
Cameron, William.
Cameron, William.
Campbell, Alexander.
Campbell, Alfred.
Campbell, Andrew.
Campbell, Angus.
Campbell, Archibald.
Campbell, Archibald.
Campbell, Archibald.
Campbell, Arthur.
Campbell, B.
Campbell, David.
Campbell, Don.
Campbell, Donald.
Campbell, George.
Campbell, G. R.
Campbell, Hugh.
Campbell, James.
Campbell, James.
Campbell, James.

Campbell, James.
Campbell, James B.
Campbell, James J.
Campbell, John.
Campbell, John.
Campbell, John.
Campbell, John.
Campbell, John.
Campbell, Joseph.
Campbell, Joseph.
Campbell, Murdoch.
Campbell, Oswald.
Campbell, Robert.
Campbell, Robert.
Campbell, William.
Campbell, William.
Campbell, William.
Canning, Alexander.
Canning, Neil.
Carmichael, James.
Carmichael, Neil.
Carolin, James.
Carr, J.
Carr, Patrick.
Carr, Patrick.

Carrick, John.
Carrol, William.
Carroll, J.
Carroll, Peter.
Carruthers, John.
Carson, Alexander.
Carson, Patrick.
Cartledge, John.
Carton, Alexander.
Cassells, John.
Cassels, Peter.
Cassidy, Charles.
Cassidy, James L.
Cassidy, Patrick.
Cassidy, Patrick.
Chalmers, James.
Chalmers, John.
Chalmers, Matthew.
Chapman, Jack.
Chasty, Edward.
Cherrie, Thomas.
Childs, Henry.
Chisholm, Robert.
Christie, Archibald.
Christie, Peter.
Clark, David.

Clark, G.
Clark, Henry.
Clark, Henry.
Clark, Hugh.
Clark, John.
Clark, Martin.
Clark, Robert.
Clark, Thomas.
Clark, Thomas.
Clark, Thomas.
Clark, Thomas.
Clark, William.
Clark, William.
Clason, Peter.
Cleare, James.
Cleare, James.
Clearie, Edward.
Cleary, John.
Clelland, Albert.
Clinton, John.
Clinton, Thomas.
Clubb, William.
Coagalton, Martin.
Cochrane, Alexander.
Cochrane, James.
Cochrane, Robert.

Cockburn, Andrew.
Colman, Smythe.
Collier, William.
Collins, James.
Collins, James.
Colquhoun, Alexander.
Colquhoun, James P.
Combe, Robert.
Conally, Robert.
Conley, John.
Conlin, John.
Connar, Pat.
Connar, Thomas.
Connor, George.
Connolly, Patrick.
Coobrough, Robert.
Coogan, Charles.
Cooke, George.
Cooke, James.
Copland, James.
Cooper, James.
Cooper, Thomas.
Cooney, James.
Cooney, Peter.
Corbett, David.
Corbett, Thomas.

Cordial, James.
Cordner, James.
Corrigan, Michael.
Corrigan, Patrick.
Costello, L.
Costello, Robert.
Costigane, Peter.
Cotterhill, Fred.
Cotton, Arthur.
Coulter, Robert.
Coulter, William.
Couper, Charles.
Couperthwaite, Robt.
Cousland, John.
Coutts, James.
Cowan, Alexander.
Cowan, Edward.
Cowan, Joseph.
Cox, Thomas.
Coyle, P.
Crabtree, Alfred.
Crabtree, Thomas.
Craig, Alexander.
Craig, J.
Craig, James.
Craig, John.

Craig, John.
Craigie, John.
Crain, Alexander.
Craken, Hugh.
Cramb, Robert.
Crawford, A.
Crawford, A.
Crawford, Byron.
Crawford, George.
Crawford, James.
Crawford, Robert.
Crawford, R. P.
Crawford, William.
Crawley, Thomas.
Cregan, Patrick.
Crichton, Alexander.
Crockett, James.
Crombie, J.
Crombie, Peter.
Crosbie, John.
Crossan, John.
Crossan, William.
Cullen, John.
Cumberland, Thomas.
Cumming, James.
Cumming, John.

Cumming, Robert.	Davenport, William.	Delacourt, Peter.	Dolan, John.
Cunningham, Alex.	Davidson, David	Derby, Patrick.	Dolan, John.
Cunningham, Eben.	Davidson, Donald.	Devine, Edward.	Dolan, John.
Cunningham, Edward.	Davidson, George.	Devlin, Edward.	Dolan, Thomas
Cunningham, Hugh.	Davidson, James.	Devlin, Harry.	Don, James.
Cunningham, J.	Davidson, James.	Dewar, William.	Donaghy, James.
Cunningham, James.	Davidson, John.	De Wit, Lambertus.	Donald, Thomas.
Cunningham, James.	Davidson, John A.	Diamond, John.	Donaldson, Alexander.
Cunningham, James G.	Davidson, William.	Dick, Andrew.	Donaldson, James.
Cunningham, John.	Davidson, William.	Dick, Andrew.	Donaldson, John.
Cunningham, John.	Davie, Charles.	Dick, John C.	Donaldson, John.
Cunningham, John L.	Davie, William.	Dickie, Robert.	Donaldson, P.
Cunningham, Robert.	Davis, James.	Dickie, William.	Donaldson, William.
Cunningham, Thomas.	Davis, R.	Dickie, William.	Donaldson, William.
Cunningham, William.	Dawson, George.	Dickson, James.	Donnachie, Charles.
Curran, John.	Dawson, William.	Dickson, Robert A.	Donnachie, William.
Currie, Angus.	Day, John.	Dillon, Thomas.	Donnan, John.
Currie, D.	Dean, James.	Dillon, Thomas.	Donnelly, Frank.
Currie, Donald.	Deans, John.	Dixon, Daniel.	Donnelly, Peter.
Currie, John.	Degning, Harry.	Docherty, Daniel.	Donnelly, Thomas.
Currie, Thomas.	Dempsey, Thomas.	Docherty, Edward.	Donnelly, Thomas.
Currie, William.	Dempster, Gilbert.	Docherty, Joseph.	Donnelly, William.
Cuthbertson, Joseph.	Dempster, Henry.	Docherty, Joseph.	Donohoe, John.
Cuthill, William.	Denniston, Samuel.	Docherty, Robert	Doohan, John.
Dalgarno, William.	Denny, George.	Docherty, William.	Dougan, John.
Darroch, John.	Denoon, David.	Doharty, James.	Dougan, Patrick J.

Douglas, Hugh.
Douglas, John.
Douglas, John.
Douglas, Robert.
Dow, Andrew.
Dow, D.
Dow, James.
Dow, Walter.
Dowie, Robert.
Downs, Charles M'Phail
Doyle, Edward.
Doyle, William.
Drake, Hugh.
Drake, William.
Drummond, E.
Drummond, John.
Drynan, R.
Drysdale, Matthew.
Drysdale, Thomas.
Duff, Alexander.
Duffin, H.
Duffy, John.
Duffy, John.
Duffy, Thomas.
Dugan, James.
Dugan, W.

Dunbar, Alexander.
Dunbar, Dan.
Dunbar, James.
Dunbar, Robert.
Dunbar, William.
Duncan, Andrew.
Duncan, Archibald.
Duncan, John.
Duncan, John.
Duncan, Robert.
Duncan, Robert.
Duncan, Thomas.
Duncan, William.
Duncanson, David.
Duncanson, G.
Dunlop, John.
Dunlop, John.
Dunlop, John.
Dunlop, Robert.
Dunn, Alexander.
Dunn, James.
Dunn, John.
Dunn, Robert.
Dunnochie, James.
Dunstone, J. A.
Dysart, J.

Eadie, William.
Easton, James.
Easton John.
Eddie, James.
Eden, John.
Edgar, Robert W.
Edgley, Fred.
Edwards, Thomas.
Edwards, Thomas.
Elborn, James.
Elliot, Hugh.
Elliot, Hugh.
Elliot, J.
Elliot, James.
Elliot, John.
Elliot, John.
Elliot, Joseph.
Elliot, Peter.
Elliot, William.
Emsley, Harry.
English, James.
Ewing, David.
Ewing, James.
Ewing, John.
Ewing, Logie.
Evans, Thoms.

Evans, Samuel.
Evans, William.
Fagan, J.
Fairgrieve, S.
Fairley, James M.
Fairley, John.
Falconer, Peter.
Fanning, James.
Fanning, Thomas.
Fanning, William.
Fannon, Patrick.
Farmer, James.
Farmer, William.
Farquhar, Walter.
Farrell, Frances.
Farrell, John.
Faulds, Frederick.
Faulds, John.
Faulds, Matthew.
Fee, James.
Fenton, Robert.
Ferguson, Alexander.
Ferguson, Alexander.
Ferguson, David.
Ferguson, Fred.
Ferguson, James.

Ferguson, James.
Ferguson, John.
Ferguson, Robert.
Ferguson, William.
Ferguson, William.
Fergusson, Cornelli.
Ferrie, Donald.
Ferrie, John.
Ferrier, Henry.
Ferriss, William.
Findlay, James.
Findlay, Robert.
Findlay, Ralph.
Finlay, William.
Finlayson, Farquhar.
Finnie, David.
Finnigan, James.
Fisackerley, George.
Fisher, Peter.
Fisken, Thomas.
Fitzpatrick, Hugh.
Fitzpatrick, Michael.
Flannigan, John.
Fleming, Archibald.
Fleming, C.
Fleming, John.

Fleming, Thomas.
Fletcher, Dawson.
Fletcher, Hugh.
Fogo, David.
Forbes, Andrew.
Forbes, Peter.
Forbes, Robert.
Forbes, William A.
Forbes, William.
Foreman, Robert.
Former, James.
Forrester, John.
Forsyth, Daniel.
Forsyth, David.
Forsyth, Robert.
Forsyth, Robert A.
Forsythe, John.
Fortune, John.
Foster, A.
Fothergill, George.
Fowler, William.
Franklin, Henry Thos.
Fraser, Alexander.
Fraser, Alexander.
Fraser, Colin.
Fraser, David.

Fraser, Donald.
Fraser, Donald.
Fraser, James S.
Fraser, John.
Fraser, Robert.
Fraser, William.
Fraser, William.
Fraser, William.
Fraser, William.
Freebairn, Archibald.
Freeburn, Thomas.
Freeman, James.
Freeman, Robert.
Friock, James.
Fullarton, Andrew.
Fullerton, Henry.
Fullerton, James.
Fullgar, Harold.
Fulton, Andrew B.
Fulton, Harry.
Fulton, Henry.
Fulton, Hugh.
Fulton, James.
Fulton, William.
Fyfe, David.
Galbraith, G.

Galbraith, William.
Gallacher, Charles.
Gallacher, D.
Gallacher, James.
Gallacher, John.
Gallacher, John.
Gallan, Alexander.
Gallic, A.
Galloway, Harold.
Gannon, Bernard.
Gardiner, Matthew.
Gardiner, Thomas.
Gardiner, William.
Gardner, H.
Gardner, James.
Gardner, Matthew.
Gardner, Robert.
Gardner, Robert.
Garrity, Henry.
Garscadden, James.
Gartley, James.
Gauley, William.
Gayne, Thomas.
Gemmell, Archibald.
Gemmell, John.
Gemmell, William.

Gerrie, George.
Gibb, Alexander.
Gibbons, Thomas.
Gibbs, A.
Gibney, Bernard.
Gibney, John.
Gibson, Andrew.
Gibson, James.
Gibson, James.
Gibson, James.
Gibson, John.
Gibson, John.
Gibson, John.
Gibson, John.
Gibson, Oliver.
Gibson, Robert.
Gibson, William.
Gibson, William.
Gieston, James.
Gilchrist, David.
Gilchrist, James.
Gilchrist, John.
Gilchrist, Peter.
Gilchrist, William.
Gilda, T.
Gillan J.

Gillan, Patrick.
Gillan, William.
Gillespie, John.
Gillespie, William.
Gillespie, W.
Gillick, Hugh.
Gillick, John.
Gillis, Alexander.
Gillis, Robert.
Gilmour, George.
Gilmour, H.
Gilmour, T.
Gilstan, James.
Gilston, Robert.
Ginn, Charles.
Girvan, John.
Glasgow, John.
Glassford, Richard.
Glen, James.
Glennie, John.
Glover, John D.
Goggins, Patrick.
Goldie, James.
Goldie, Peter.
Goodall, John.
Goodman, Hugh.

Goodman, Thomas.
Gordon, James.
Gordon, John.
Gordon, P.
Gorham, James.
Gorman, John.
Gorman, William.
Gosland, Allan.
Goudie, William.
Gow, Alexander.
Graham, Alex.
Graham, David.
Graham, D.
Graham, James.
Graham, John.
Graham, John.
Graham, J.
Graham, R.
Graham, Thomas.
Graham, Thomas.
Graham, William.
Graney, Law.
Grant, A.
Grant, George.
Grant, Hugh.
Grant, James.

Grant, M.
Gray, David.
Gray, Henry.
Gray, James.
Gray, John.
Greenlees, Walter.
Greer, Charles.
Grew, William.
Greig, David.
Greig, James.
Greig, William.
Gribbon, Henry.
Gribbon, Hugh.
Grierson, Matt.
Griffen, John.
Groundwater, J.
Groves, David.
Gunn, William.
Gunning, James D.
Guthrie, Hugh.
Guthrie, John.
Guy, John.
Guy, Robert.
Haddow, George.
Haddow, James.
Hain, Andrew.

Hair, Adam.	Hamilton, Matthew.	Haugh, James.	Hendry, Harry.
Hair, Adam P.	Hamilton, Samuel.	Haveron, T.	Hendry, James.
Hair, Hugh.	Hancox, Frank.	Hay, John.	Hendry, John.
Hair, James.	Hancox, Frank.	Hay, Robert.	Hendry, John.
Halford, Samuel.	Hanley, Charles.	Hay, Robert.	Hendry, Neil.
Hall, J.	Hanlin, Thomas.	Hay, Robert.	Hendry, Patrick.
Hall, Thomas.	Hannah, Ben.	Healy, Thomas.	Hendry, Robert.
Halley, John.	Hannah, John.	Healy, William.	Henny, George.
Halliday, Harry.	Hannah, John.	Heath, Arthur.	Henry, David.
Hallidey, John.	Hannah, Samuel.	Hefan, Charles.	Henshilwood, Andrew.
Halliday, J.	Hannah, Samuel.	Heggie, Robert.	Hepburn, Alexander.
Halliday, William.	Hannay, Douglas.	Hemphill, John.	Hepburn, Andrew.
Hamil, Robert.	Hannon, J.	Henderson, Alexander.	Hepburn, J.
Hamilton, Alexander.	Hare, Andrew.	Henderson, Charles.	Hepburn, Robert.
Hamilton, A.	Harper, Samuel.	Henderson, David.	Hepburn, Stewart.
Hamilton, Charles.	Harris, George.	Henderson, Donald.	Heraty, Richard.
Hamilton, Charles.	Harris, James.	Henderson, D.	Heraty, Walter.
Hamilton, David.	Harrison, Joseph.	Henderson, James.	Herbert, John.
Hamilton, David.	Hart, Thomas.	Henderson, James.	Heron, Philip.
Hamilton, George.	Harte, George.	Henderson, John.	Herriot, Arthur.
Hamilton, Hugh.	Harton, Denis.	Henderson, Robert.	Heylands, Hercules.
Hamilton, James.	Harvey, M.	Henderson, Robert.	Hickey, John.
Hamilton, James.	Hastie, Walter.	Henderson, Robert.	Higgins, James.
Hamilton, James.	Hastings, C.	Henderson, W.	Higgins, James.
Hamilton, John.	Hatchwell, Alexander.	Hendry, Alexander.	Higgins, John.
Hamilton, J.	Hattrick, Alexander.	Hendry, Andrew.	Hilder, F.

Hill, George.
Hill, George W.
Hill, James.
Hodgkinson, William J.
Hoey, Robert.
Hogarth, John.
Holmes, Alexander.
Holmes, C.
Holmes, John.
Honeyford, W.
Hood, Douglas.
Hood, Robert.
Hood, William.
Hopkins, Daniel.
Hopkirk, Robert.
Hopper, John.
Horgan, Andrew.
Horne, David B.
Hosie, James.
Hosie, James Nixon.
Hosie, John.
Hoskins, George.
Houston, Adam.
Houston, James.
Houston, William.
Houston, William.

Howard, Edward.
Howat, John.
Howey, W. J.
Howie, Francis.
Howie, William.
Hubbick, Alfred.
Hughes, Arthur.
Hughes, James.
Hughes, James.
Hughes, John.
Hughes, John.
Hughes, William.
Hunter, Alexander.
Hunter, David.
Hunter, D.
Hunter, George.
Hunter, George.
Hunter, George.
Hunter, George A.
Hunter, John.
Hunter, J. T.
Hunter, William.
Hunter, William.
Hunter, William.
Hunter, William.
Huntly, James.

Hurrell, Robert.
Hutcheson, David.
Hutcheson, James.
Hutchison, Andrew.
Hutchison, James.
Hutchison, John.
Hutchison, Robert.
Hutchison, William.
Hutton, Duncan.
Hynes, J. H.
Hyslop, Gavin.
Hyslop, John.
Hyslop, Robert.
Inglis, Robert.
Inglis, Thomas.
Innes, Alfred.
Innes, Gordon.
Innes, Herbert.
Innes, James.
Innes, John.
Ironside, H.
Irvine, David H.
Irvine, George.
Irvine, James A.
Irvine, John.
Irvine, Robert.

Irvine, William.
Irving, Fergus.
Ivory, Thomas.
Jack, Alexander.
Jack, Hugh.
Jack, James.
Jack, John.
Jack, Peter.
Jackson, Joseph.
Jackson, Samuel.
James, Robert.
Jamieson, Daniel.
Jardine, Peter.
Jarvis, J.
Jeffrey, John.
Jeffrey, Robert.
Jenkins, Peter.
Jenkins, W.
Johnston, Adam.
Johnston, Albert.
Johnston, Frank.
Johnston, George.
Johnston, John.
Johnston, John.
Johnston, Lamont.
Johnstone, Alexander.

Johnstone, Angus.	Kay, James.	Kennedy, John.	King, John.
Johnstone, David.	Kay, Robert.	Kennedy, Martin.	King, Joseph.
Johnstone, Frank.	Kay, William.	Kennedy, Richard.	King, William.
Johnstone, James.	Keady, J.	Kennedy, Thomas.	King, William.
Johnstone, James.	Kean, James.	Kennedy, William.	King, W.
Johnstone, James.	Keegan, P.	Kenny, John.	Kinloch, James.
Johnstone, James.	Keir, John.	Kerr, Andrew.	Kinnon, John.
Johnstone, James.	Kellary, Michael.	Kerr, Edward.	Kirby, James.
Johnstone, James W.	Kelly, Denis.	Kerr, James.	Kirk, William.
Johnstone, John.	Kelly, George.	Kerr, James.	Kirker, Alexander.
Johnstone, John.	Kelly, James.	Kerr, James.	Kirkland, Hugh.
Johnstone, John.	Kelly, James.	Kerr, John.	Kirkland, Tom.
Johnstone, Joseph.	Kelly, James.	Kerr, J.	Kirkpatrick, Fred.
Johnstone, Joseph.	Kelly, John.	Kerr, J.	Kirkwood, Archibald.
Johnstone, Thomas.	Kelly, John.	Kerr, Robert.	Kirkwood, Richard.
Johnstone, William.	Kelly, John.	Kerr, Robert.	Kivney, J.
Johnstone, William.	Kelly, John.	Kesley, Andrew.	Knox, James.
Jones, Henry.	Kelly, Patrick.	Kidd, James.	Koch, C.
Jones, William.	Kelly, Richard.	Kiddle, Robert.	Koch, James.
Jones, William.	Kelly, William.	Kiernan, Patrick.	Laidlaw, Thomas.
Jordan, James.	Kelly, William.	Kilcullen, Daniel.	Laing, Robert.
Jordan, Peter.	Kemp, Robert.	Kilgour, Peter.	Laird, Robert.
Kain, Robert.	Kempen, Edward.	Kilpatrick, William.	Lally, John.
Kane, John.	Kenna, Michael.	Kincaid, William.	Lamb, William.
Kay, David.	Kennedy, James.	King, Alexander.	Lamb, William.
	Kennedy, John.		Lambert, John.

Lambert, William.
Lambert, William.
Lamond, Frederick.
Lamond, John.
Lamond, Neil.
Lamont, David.
Lamont, John.
Lang, Henry.
Laurence, James.
Laurence, John.
Laverie, Alexander.
Law, Andrew.
Law, Robert.
Law, Thomas.
Lawrence, James.
Lawson, John.
Lawson, Robert.
Learmonth, G.
Leckie, James.
Lee, Andrew.
Lee, William.
Lees, Percy.
Leith, James.
Lennon, James.
Lennox, Harry.
Lennox, Wilson.

Leslie, James.
Lewis, Alexander.
Lewis, John.
Lewis, John.
Liddell, Neil.
Liddell, William.
Lillie, Andrew.
Lindsay, George.
Lindsay, James.
Lindsay, Thomas.
Lindsay, William.
Linton, Harry.
Lipsett, Patrick.
Lister, James.
Little, Archibald.
Little, Joseph.
Little, Wilfred.
Livingstone, George.
Livingstone, J.
Livingstone, William.
Livsey, J.
Loan, James.
Lochhead, Alexander.
Lochhead, Robert.
Lockhart, Alfred.
Logan, James.

Logan, R.
Lone, Henry.
Lone, Joseph.
Long, James.
Long, James F.
Longridge, Warnock.
Loughrey, James.
Lovatt, Joseph.
Love, Hugh N.
Love, James.
Love, John.
Love, J.
Love, Richard.
Luke, Hugh.
Luke, William.
Lumley, John.
Lunn, Charles.
Lynch, John.
Lynch, Michael.
Lynch, Patrick.
Lynd, James.
Lyon, Andrew.
Lyon, Robert.
M'Adoo, James.
M'Allister, Alexander.
M'Allister, Daniel.

M'Allister, George.
M'Allister, John.
M'Aloon, Patrick.
M'Ara, James.
M'Ard, James.
M'Arthur, Donald.
M'Arthur, Don. M'D.
M'Arthur, Neil.
M'Ateer, Charles.
M'Aulay, Edward.
M'Aulay, James.
M'Aulay, Samuel.
M'Anlay, S.
M'Aulay, Thomas.
M'Aulay, Thomas.
M'Aulay, William.
M'Ausland, John.
M'Auslane, J. B.
M'Bean, Victor.
M'Beth, John.
M'Bride, Charles.
M'Bride, Daniel.
M'Bride, John.
M'Bride, Samuel.
M'Cabe, Dominic.
M'Caffrey, William P.

M'Call, David.
M'Call, Robert.
M'Call, William.
M'Callum, Alexander.
M'Callum, Daniel.
M'Callum, Hugh.
M'Callum, J.
M'Callum, Robert.
M'Cam, Benjamin.
M'Cann, James.
M'Cann, Patrick.
M'Caskill, John.
M'Carroll, E.
M'Clement, William.
M'Cloy, Hugh.
M'Clay, William.
M'Cluckie, Alexander.
M'Colgan, Francis.
M'Coll, John.
M'Coll, Robert.
M'Comish, Edward.
M'Comish, William.
M'Connell, David.
M'Cool, J.
M'Cormack, George.
M'Cormack, George.

M'Cormack, John.
M'Cormack, Thomas.
M'Cormack, T.
M'Cormack, William.
M'Cormick, M.
M'Cormick, Stephen.
M'Creadie, Robert.
M'Crorie, Henry.
M'Cudden, Daniel.
M'Cue, John.
M'Culloch, Hans.
M'Culloch, Harry.
M'Culloch, Hugh.
M'Culloch, James.
M'Culloch, James.
M'Culloch, John.
M'Culloch, Robert.
M'Culloch, Stewart.
M'Cully, Thomas.
M'Cutcheon, J.
M'Dade, Edward.
M'Dade, James.
M'Dade, John.
M'Dermid, Archibald.
M'Dermott, Hugh.
M'Dermott, Michael.

M'Diarmid, Andrew.
M'Diarmid, Thomas.
M'Donald, Alexander.
M'Donald, Alexander.
M'Donald, Charles.
M'Donald, Donald.
M'Donald, Donald.
M'Donald, George.
M'Donald, George.
M'Donald, George.
M'Donald, Gilbert.
M'Donald, James.
M'Donald, James.
M'Donald, John.
M'Donald, John.
M'Donald, John.
M'Donald, John.
M'Donald, J. B.
M'Donald, Murdo.
M'Donald, Norman.
M'Donald, N.
M'Donald, Wm. L.
M'Donald, William.
M'Dougall, Hugh.
M'Dougall, Robert.
M'Dowall, James.

M'Dowall, John.
M'Elroy, Peter.
M'Ewan, Andrew.
M'Ewan, David.
M'Ewan, James.
M'Ewan, Samuel.
M'Fadden, James.
M'Fadyen, Stephen.
M'Farlane, Alexander.
M'Farlane, Alexander.
M'Farlane, Alexander.
M'Farlane, Archibald.
M'Farlane, A.
M'Farlane, Daniel.
M'Farlane, G.
M'Farlane, James.
M'Farlane, James.
M'Farlane, James.
M'Farlane, John.
M'Farlane, John.
M'Farlane, John.
M'Farlane, J.
M'Farlane, J.
M'Farlane, Neil.
M'Farlane, Robert.
M'Farlane, Robert.

M'Farlane, Robert.	M'Govern, James.	M'Guire, Charles.	M'Intyre, Archibald.
M'Farlane, Robert.	M'Govern, Patrick.	M'Guire, Edward.	M'Intyre, Archibald.
M'Farlane, William.	M'Gowan, P.	M'Guire, George.	M'Intyre, George.
M'Farlane, William K.	M'Gowan, P.	M'Guire, George.	M'Intyre, James.
M'Garrigle, Robert.	M'Gowan, W.	M'Guire, Hector.	M'Intyre, James.
M'Garvie, Andrew.	M'Granthin, Walter.	M'Guire, John.	M'Intyre, Peter.
M'Geachy, Wm. Stalker.	M'Graw, William.	M'Guire, Joseph.	M'Intyre, Thomas.
M'Geady, Joseph A.	M'Gregor, Alexander.	M'Guire, Patrick.	M'Intyre, William.
M'Geeghan, John.	M'Gregor, Anthony.	M'Gurgen, James.	M'Ivor, John.
M'Geehin, John.	M'Gregor, Archibald.	M'Hardy, James.	M'Kay, Allan.
M'Geehin, Peter.	M'Gregor, A.	M'Ilroy, Alexander.	M'Kay, Aulay.
M'Gettigan, William.	M'Gregor, Daniel.	M'Ilvain, Archibald.	M'Kay, Donald.
M'Ghie, Samuel.	M'Gregor, Donald.	M'Ilvanie, Andrew.	Mackay, Duncan.
M'Gibbon, Samuel.	M'Gregor, Donald.	M'Ilwraith, Robert.	M'Kay, James.
M'Gill, Hugh.	M'Gregor, Gregor.	M'Ilwraith, William.	M'Kay, Robert.
M'Gill, James.	M'Gregor, James.	M'Inally, John.	M'Kay, Tom.
M'Gill, John.	M'Gregor, James.	M'Innes, George.	M'Kay, William.
M'Ginn, Richard.	M'Gregor, John.	M'Innes, James.	M'Kay, William.
M'Ginnes, Neil.	M'Gregor, John.	M'Innes, William.	M'Kean, William.
M'Glashan, Donald.	M'Gregor, Joseph.	M'Innes, William.	M'Kean, William.
M'Goff, James.	M'Gregor, Norman.	M'Intosh, James.	M'Keand, John.
M'Goff, John.	M'Gregor, Peter.	M'Intosh, John.	M'Kechnie, George.
M'Goldrick, John.	M'Gregor, Stewart.	M'Intosh, Robert.	M'Kechnie, John.
M'Goldrick, Philip.	M'Gregor, Thomas.	M'Intosh, William.	M'Kee, James.
M'Gonigle, John.	M'Guinnes, Michael.	Mackintosh, Alex.	M'Kee, James.
M'Gonnell, Edward.	M'Guinnes, Thomas.	M'Intyre, Archibald.	M'Kell, Archibald.

M'Kellar, William.
M'Kelvie, Matthew.
M'Kendrick, Thomas.
M'Kenna, David.
M'Kenna, William.
M'Kenzie, Allan.
M'Kenzie, Charles.
M'Kenzie, Ewen.
M'Kenzie, George.
M'Kenzie, John.
M'Kenzie, John.
M'Kenzie, John F.
M'Kenzie, J.
M'Kenzie, Kenneth.
M'Kenzie, Peter.
M'Kenzie, Robert.
M'Kenzie, Thomas
M'Keown, James.
M'Kernan, David.
M'Kernan, John.
Mackie, James.
Mackie, Thomas.
M'Killin, William.
M'Kimm, Robert.
M'Kinlay, Andrew.
M'Kinnon, Alexander.

M'Kinnon, Colin.
M'Kinnon, Donald.
M'Kinnon, Peter.
M'Kirdy, Andrew.
M'Lachlan, Archibald.
M'Lachlan, Donald.
M'Lachlan, Hugh.
M'Lachlan, H.
M'Lachlan, James.
M'Lachlan, William.
M'Lafferty, George.
M'Lafferty, John.
M'Lancy, Robert.
M'Laney, William.
M'Laren, David.
M'Laren, George.
M'Laren, George.
M'Laren, Joseph.
M'Larty, John.
M'Laughlin, Bernard.
M'Laughlin, George.
M'Laughlin, Hugh.
M'Laughlin, James.
M'Laughlin, John.
M'Laughlin, L.
M'Laughlin, R.

M'Lay, Andrew.
M'Lean, James.
M'Lean, James.
M'Lean, John.
M'Lean, Joseph.
M'Lean, Joseph.
M'Lean, Laughlan.
M'Lean, Norman.
M'Lean, Robert.
M'Lean, Stephen.
M'Leary, John.
M'Lellan, Charles.
M'Lellan, William.
M'Lelland, Alexander.
M'Lelland, James.
M'Lennan, John.
M'Lennan, Kenneth.
M'Lennan, William.
M'Leod, Angus.
M'Leod, George.
M'Leod, Hugh.
M'Leod, John.
M'Leod, Peter.
M'Leod, William.
M'Lorn, G.
M'Lure, John.

M'Mahon, John.
M'Manus, Frank.
M'Manus, George.
M'Manus, John.
M'Master, James.
M'Meel, James.
M'Millan, Archibald.
M'Millan, Edward.
M'Millan, James.
M'Millan, James.
M'Millan, John.
M'Millan, John.
M'Millan, John.
M'Millan, John.
M'Millan, Richard.
M'Millan, William.
M'Millan, William.
M'Murdo, James.
M'Murray, Michael.
M'Nab, William.
M'Nair, James.
M'Nair, John.
M'Naught, Jacob Brown.
M'Naught, Thomas.
M'Nay, Samuel

29

M'Neil, Alexander.
M'Neil, James.
M'Neil, James.
M'Neil, John.
M'Neill, John.
M'Neill, Robert.
M'Neilly, William.
M'Nelio, Francis.
M'Nie, John.
M'Nicol, Archibald.
M'Nicol, Archibald.
M'Nicol, Donald.
M'Nicol, Hugh.
M'Niven, Angus.
M'Niven, Duncan.
M'Niven, Duncan.
M'Niven, John.
M'Phail, Donald.
M'Phee, Donald.
M'Pherson, Duncan.
M'Pherson, Duncan.
M'Pherson, James.
M'Pherson, J.
M'Pherson, Robert.
M'Pherson, Samuel.
M'Pherson, William.

M'Quade, Edwin.
M'Quade, Robert.
M'Quat, Andrew.
M'Quat, Thomas.
M'Quattie, Charles.
M'Queen, John.
M'Queen, J.
M'Quillan, George.
M'Quillan, P.
M'Reynolds, William.
M'Roberts, Samuel.
M'Shea, Andrew.
M'Sorley, John.
M'Taggart, Robert.
M'Vey, William.
M'Whirr, James.
M'Whirr, J.
M'William, Adam.
M'William, R.
M'Williams, John.
Magee, Robert.
Mahaffie, William.
Major, James.
Major, W.
Malloch, George.
Malonie, Peter.

Manley, Charles.
Manson, Andrew.
Marley, Hugh.
Marnie, Norman.
Marshall, Andrew.
Marshall, Colin.
Marshall, David.
Marshall, James.
Marshall, James.
Marshall, John.
Marshall, John.
Marshall, Samuel.
Marshall, Thomas.
Martin, James.
Martin, John.
Martin, John M.
Martin, Joseph.
Martin, Peter.
Martin, Stephen J.
Martin, Thomas.
Marvis, Alexander.
Mason, John.
Massie, Marianus.
Masterton, William.
Matheson, Donald.
Mathie, Robert.

Mathieson, Hugh.
Mathieson, John.
Matthews, Richard.
Mauchlin, John.
Maxwell, Neil.
Maxwell, William.
Mealyea, Henry.
Mearns, Archibald.
Meffen, John.
Meikle, James.
Meldrum, Robert.
Meldrum, Thomas.
Meldrum, Thomas.
Mellon, Edward.
Mellon, John.
Melville, William.
Melvin, John.
Mercer, John.
Merrilees, George.
Merry, Archibald.
Merry, James.
Michie, Samuel.
Mill, Philip.
Millaney, Peter.
Millar, Alexander.
Millar, Andrew B.

Millar, John.
Millar, Joseph.
Miller, Alexander.
Miller, Arthur A.
Miller, A.
Miller, Charles.
Miller, David.
Miller, David.
Miller, Donald M.
Miller, D.
Miller, Edwin.
Miller, James.
Miller, John.
Miller, John.
Miller, Robert.
Miller, R.
Miller, T.
Milligan, David.
Milliken, John.
Milmoe, Charles.
Milne, Thomas.
Milne, William.
Milroy, P.
Mirner, Edward.
Mitchell, Charles.
Mitchell, Daniel.

Mitchell, Hugh.
Mitchell, James.
Mitchell, Robert.
Mochan, Charles.
Mochnie, William.
Moffatt, J.
Moffatt, William.
Moir, Alexander.
Moir, David.
Moir, Frank.
Moir, W.
Monaghan, Charles.
Monaghan, D.
Mongo, Thomas.
Monk, John.
Montgomerie, David.
Montgomerie, John.
Montgomery, Andrew
Montgomery, Charles.
Montgomery, Charles.
Montgomery, David.
Montgomery, David.
Montgomery, Robert.
Montgomery, Wm. G.
Moodie, D.
Moodie, John.

Mooney. Pat.
Mooney, Patrick.
Moore, Albert.
Moore, Francis.
Moore, Thomas.
Moore, William.
Moran, Patrick.
Moran, William.
Morgan, Arthur.
Morgan, George.
Morgan, Gilbert.
Morris, Arthur.
Morrison, Alexander.
Morrison, Archibald.
Morrison, Charles.
Morrison, Charles.
Morrison, George.
Morrison, John.
Morrison, Norman.
Morrison, Peter.
Morrison, William.
Morrow, William.
Morton, Andrew.
Morton, A.
Morton, Gavin.
Morton, James.

Mouat, Alexander.
Moyies, David.
Muir, A.
Muir, Edward.
Muir, George.
Muir, James.
Muir, James.
Muir, John.
Muir, William.
Muirhead, John B.
Muirhead, Robert.
Mulholland, John.
Mulholland, William.
Mulholland, William.
Munro, Alexander.
Munro, Alexander.
Munro, David.
Munro, Frank.
Munro, John.
Murdoch, Alex. Inslee.
Murdoch, John.
Murdoch, Robert.
Murdoch, Samuel.
Murdoch, Stewart.
Murphy, Charles.
Murphy, Ernest.

Murphy, James.
Murphy, John.
Murphy, John.
Murphy, John.
Murphy, John.
Murphy, Thomas.
Murphy, W.
Murray, Alexander.
Murray, Archibald.
Murray, Andrew.
Murray, David.
Murray, Hugh.
Murray, James.
Murray, James.
Murray, John.
Murray, John.
Murray, John B.
Murray, Patrick.
Murray, Peter.
Murray, Thomas.
Naismith, Thomas.
Nairn, Andrew.
Nairn, John.
Neil, Robert.
Neil, Samuel.
Neil, Thomas.

Neillie, John.
Neilly, John.
Neilson, George.
Neilson, James.
Neilson, John P.
Nelson, Samuel.
Nesbit, M'Whirter.
Nichol, Alexander.
Nichol, William.
Nicholson, Malcolm.
Nicholson, Matthew.
Nicholson, Matthew.
Nicholson, Robert.
Nicol, John.
Nicol, William.
Nicolson, Robert.
Nimmo, Alexander.
Niven, Daniel.
Niven, Peter.
Nixon, Fred.
Nixon, James.
Nixon, James.
Nixon, Robert.
Nixon, William.
Notman, Robert.
O'Brien, John.

O'Connor, Hugh.
O'Connor, James.
O'Donnell, Hugh.
O'Donnell, Hugh.
O'Donnell, James.
O'Donnell, Maurice.
O'Hare, Michael.
O'Kane, James.
O'Lone, John.
O'Malley, Michael.
O'Malley, Patrick.
O'Neill, Francis.
O'Neil, Edward.
O'Neil, Edward.
O'Neil, Hugh.
Ogilvie, James.
Ogilvie, Peter.
Oliver, George.
Oliver, Robert.
Oliver, Thomas.
Oliver, William.
Orme, Robert.
Orr, Robert.
Orrell, Thomas.
Osborne, John.
Ovens, David.

Overend, James.
Overend, James.
Owens, William.
Owens, Charles.
Paisley, John.
Park, Henry.
Park, James.
Park, J.
Park, Robert.
Park, Thomas.
Park, William.
Parr, J.
Pate, Hugh.
Paterson, Alexander.
Paterson, Gavin.
Paterson, Gavin.
Paterson, George.
Paterson, George.
Paterson, George.
Paterson, James.
Paterson, John.
Paterson, John.
Paterson, John.
Paterson, Robert.
Paterson, Robert.
Paterson, Robert.

Paterson, Robert G.	Phillips Samuel.	Preston, John.	Reid, David.
Paterson, W.	Phillips, William.	Pritchard, Charles.	Reid, George.
Paterson, W.	Pierce, Alexander.	Proctor, David.	Reid, Harry.
Paton, A.	Pinkerton, George.	Provan, Alexander.	Reid, Hugh.
Paton, H. J.	Pirie, George.	Provan, John.	Reid, James.
Paton, James.	Platen, Peter.	Quigley, John.	Reid, James.
Paton, Robert.	Polland, John.	Quinn, Frank.	Reid, John.
Paton, Thomas.	Pollock, George.	Quinn, James.	Reid, John
Patrick, Johnston.	Pollock, John.	Rae, George.	Reid, Peter.
Pattison, Henry.	Pollock, Robert.	Raeburn, James.	Reid, Robert.
Paul, James.	Pollock, Robert.	Rain, John.	Reid, Robert.
Payne, George.	Pollock, Thomas.	Raitt, G.	Reid, Robert.
Peacock, George.	Pope, Charles.	Ramsay, Alexander.	Reid, Robert.
Peden, Robert.	Porrie, James.	Ramsay, James.	Reid, Samuel.
Penman, John.	Porter, William.	Ramsay, John.	Reid, William.
Penman, John.	Porteous, Peter.	Ramsay, W. J.	Reid, William.
Penman, Robert.	Porteous, Peter.	Rankin, T.	Reilly, Frank.
Perston, William.	Porteous, Thomas.	Rankin, William.	Reilly, John.
Peterkin, Robert.	Porteous, Thomas.	Reavey, Alexander.	Reilly, John.
Peters, Frederick.	Potts, John.	Reeves, Robert.	Reilly, Patrick.
Pettigrew, Alexander.	Powrie, William.	Reid, Alexander.	Renfrew, Findlay
Phelan, Thomas.	Prentice, D.	Reid, Alexander.	Rennie, William.
Philip, Joseph.	Prentice, James.	Reid, Alexander.	Renton, George.
Phillips, Arthur.	Presse, William.	Reid, Alexander.	Renton, Richard.
Phillips, Henry.	Preston, David	Reid, Charles.	Renton, Thomas.
Phillips, Robert.	Preston, James.	Reid, Crawford.	Renwick, Frank.

Revie, William.
Reynolds, Richard.
Rice, James.
Richmond, Alexander.
Richmond, David.
Richmond, James C.
Riddell, James.
Riddell, John.
Riddell, Roderick.
Riddell, Walter.
Riggs, John Henry.
Rintoul, John.
Ritchie, Robert.
Robb, Colin.
Robb, Robert.
Roberts, Alexander.
Roberts, Thomas.
Robertson, Alexander.
Robertson, Andrew.
Robertson, David.
Robertson, Don.
Robertson, George.
Robertson, Hugh.
Robertson, James.
Robertson, James.
Robertson, James.

Robertson, John.
Robertson, John.
Robertson, John.
Robertson, John.
Robertson, John J.
Robertson, Peter.
Robertson, William.
Robertson, W.
Robin, Andrew.
Robins, F.
Robinson, George.
Roddy, John.
Rodger, James.
Rodgers, James.
Rodgers, John.
Rodgers, John.
Roe, Michael.
Rogers, Peter.
Rollo, D.
Rollo, W.
Ronald, Archibald.
Rooney, B. A.
Ross, Alexander.
Ross, Allan.
Ross, Charles.
Ross, Charles.

Ross, Colin.
Ross, James.
Ross, John.
Ross, Joseph E.
Ross, J.
Ross, William.
Rough, Robert.
Rowat, Thomas.
Rowan, James.
Rush, Charles.
Russell, Allan.
Russell, G. B.
Russell, John W.
Russell, John.
Russell, Lenoard.
Russell, William.
Russell, William.
Rutherford, Robert.
Ryan, William.
Salter, William.
Samuels, David.
Sanderson, George.
Sandills, Sydney D.
Sands, Robert.
Saunders, John.
Savage, Hugh.

Savage, James.
Sawyer, H.
Schofield, Alexander.
Schofield, Sidney M.
Sconnell, Lawrence.
Scott, James.
Scott, John.
Scott, Peter.
Scott, Thomas.
Scott, William.
Seaward, Henry.
Sellars, James.
Sergeant, Thomas.
Sergeant, Walter.
Shankland, Robert.
Shannon, James.
Shannon, William.
Sharp, Alexander.
Sharp, James.
Sharp, James B.
Sharp, Robert.
Sharp, Robert S.
Shaw, Alexander.
Shaw, Donald.
Shaw, Robert.
Shaw, Thomas.

Shaw, T.	Sinclair, Robert.	Smith, Harry.	Spence, Peter.
Shearer, Edward.	Sinclair, William.	Smith, James.	Spence, William.
Shearer, George.	Skinner, Alexander.	Smith, James.	Spratt, Patrick.
Shearer, William.	Skinner, George.	Smith, James.	Springate, C.
Sheldon, Thomas.	Skinner, George.	Smith, James.	Springate, John.
Sheppard, James.	Skinner, John.	Smith, James.	Stainton, Samuel.
Sheridan, Thomas.	Slater, A.	Smith, James M.	Stangee, Thomas.
Sheridan, William.	Slavin, W. J.	Smith, John.	Starrs, James.
Shields, Robert.	Sloan, Bryce.	Smith, John.	Steel, Samuel.
Shields, Rodger.	Sloan, Robert.	Smith, John M.	Steel, William.
Shirlaw, William.	Sloan, Thomas.	Smith, Robert.	Stein, William.
Short, John.	Sloan, William.	Smith, Thomas.	Stephen, James.
Short, Thomas.	Sloan, William.	Smith, Thomas.	Stevenson, Alexander.
Shreenan, Charles.	Slowey, Arthur.	Smith, Thomas.	Stevenson, Alfred.
Shuttleton, William	Small, Bruce.	Smith, William.	Stevenson, Henry.
Sim, John.	Smart, James.	Smith, William.	Stevenson, James.
Simpson, Alexander.	Smart, John.	Smith, William.	Stevenson, John.
Simpson, Andrew.	Smart, Ritchie M.	Smith, William.	Stevenson, John.
Simpson, Andrew.	Smith, Alexander.	Smith, William.	Stevenson, Thomas.
Simpson, Charles.	Smith, Allan.	Smith, William G.	Stevenson, T.
Simpson, Peter.	Smith, A.	Smyth, Charles.	Stevenson, Walter.
Simpson, Thomas.	Smith, Clement.	Smyth, William.	Stevenson, William.
Simpson, William.	Smith, Daniel.	Sneddon, James.	Stewart, Alexander.
Simpson, William.	Smith, Duncan.	Soder, Henry.	Stewart, Alfred.
Sinclair, James.	Smith, George.	Sommerville, Daniel.	Stewart, Duncan.
Sinclair, Peter.	Smith, George.	Speirs, James.	Stewart, Hugh.

Stewart, James.	Summers, Finlay.	Taylor, James.	Thomson, George.
Stewart, James.	Summers, John.	Taylor, James.	Thomson, George.
Stewart, James.	Surgenor, Neil.	Taylor, James.	Thomson, George H.
Stewart, James C.	Sutherland, Hugh.	Taylor, John.	Thomson, Harry.
Stewart, John.	Sutherland, John.	Taylor, John.	Thomson, Hugh.
Stewart, John.	Swan, James.	Taylor, Peter.	Thomson, James.
Stewart, John.	Swan, Peter.	Taylor, Peter.	Thomson, James.
Stewart, Joseph.	Sweeney, Andrew.	Taylor, Robert.	Thomson, James.
Stewart, Lyle.	Sweeney, Edmund.	Taylor, Robert.	Thomson, John.
Stewart, William.	Sweeney, Thomas.	Taylor, Thomas.	Thomson, John.
Stewart, William.	Sweeney, William.	Taylor, William.	Thomson, John.
Stewart, William.	Symes, John Roy.	Taylor, William.	Thomson, John H.
Stewart, William.	Tabor, James.	Telford, William.	Thomson, Richard.
Stimpson, Richard.	Tacey, Joseph.	Temple, Thomas.	Thomson, Robert.
Stirling, Andrew.	Taggart, Isaac.	Tennant, Thomas.	Thomson, R.
Stobo, James.	Taggart, Thomas.	Tennant William.	Thomson, Samuel.
Stoddart, John.	Tait, Charles.	Terrace, David.	Thomson, Thomas.
Storey, William.	Tait, James.	Terry, Robert.	Thomson, Thomas.
Stower, Thomas.	Tait, James.	Thayne, John.	Thomson, William.
Strachan, Robert.	Tait, James.	Third, John.	Thomson, William.
Straine, D.	Tait, Robert.	Thompson, James.	Thomson, William.
Strang, John.	Taylor, David.	Thompson, Peter.	Tidd, J
Stretch, Andrew.	Taylor, Edward.	Thompson, Robert.	Tierney, James.
Struthers, John.	Taylor, Gavin D.	Thomson, Andrew.	Timoney, Charles.
Sturrock, George.	Taylor, George.	Thomson, Charles.	Timoney, John.
Sulivan, James.	Taylor, George B.	Thomson, David.	Toal, Patrick.

36

Todd, John.	Urquhart, Thomas.	Ward, James.	Weir, Dougal
Todd, William.	Urquhart, William.	Ward, Richard.	Weir, John.
Todd, William.	Valentine, George.	Ward, Thomas.	Weir, Robert.
Tolland, William.	Vallance, J.	Wardlaw, Benjamin.	Weir, William.
Torrance, J.	Vallance, Robert.	Wardrop, A.	Welsh, Hugh.
Torrance, J.	Vance, John.	Wark, James.	Welsh, James.
Tosh, John.	Vaughan, David.	Warren, Ronald.	Welsh, William.
Townley, John.	Vogwill, Robert.	Waterson, John.	Welsh, William.
Train, Alexander.	Waddell, James.	Watson, Angus.	West, Charles.
Train, John.	Waddell, John.	Watson, David.	Westwater, Alexander.
Trainer, Andrew.	Waddell, Robert.	Watson, D.	Wheelans, James.
Travers, Andrew.	Wales, James.	Watson, George.	Wheeler, Mark.
Travers, Thomas.	Walker, A.	Watson, John.	White, John.
Troughton, Francis.	Walker, Hugh.	Watson, John.	White, Richard.
Troughton, Frank.	Walker, James.	Watson, Robert.	White, Robert.
Turnbull, James.	Walker, John.	Watson, Robert.	White, Thomas B.
Turnbull, James.	Walker, Robert.	Watson, R.	White, William.
Turnbull, Thomas.	Walker, R.	Watson, Thomas B.	White, William.
Turner, Alexander.	Wallace, David.	Watson, Walter.	White, William James.
Turner, Robert.	Wallace, David.	Watson, William.	Whitehill, D.
Turner, S.	Walsh, John.	Watt, Alexander.	Whitelaw, Archibald.
Tyrell, Hamilton.	Walters, William.	Watt, George.	Whitelaw, Dugald.
Tyrell, Michael.	Wands, Robert.	Watt, Thomas.	Whitelaw, James.
Ure, Adam.	Wanless, A.	Webster, Farquhar.	Whitelaw, Thomas.
Ure, John.	Wapshaw, Ebenezer.	Wegg, John.	Whitelaw, William.
Ure, William.	Ward, George.	Weir, Alexander.	Whiteside, Walter.

Whitler, James E.
Whitton, Peter.
Wiggins, William.
Wilcock, Stanley.
Wilkie, H. G.
Wilkie, John.
Williamson, Alexander.
Wilson, Alexander.
Wilson, Alexander.
Wilson, Hugh.
Wilson, James.
Wilson, James.
Wilson, James.
Wilson, James.
Wilson, John.
Wilson, Kennedy.
Wilson, Matthew.

Wilson, Robert.
Wilson, Robert.
Wilson, Robert.
Wilson, Samuel.
Wilson, Thomas.
Wilson, Thomas.
Wilson, William.
Winning, John.
Winning, William.
Winter, Henry.
Winter, Robert.
Winter, Thomas.
Winton, Alexander
Winton, James.
Wood, Alexander.
Wood, William.
Wood, W. E.

Woodrow, Duncan.
Wright, Albert.
Wright, Alexander.
Wright, Archibald.
Wright, Francis.
Wright, James
Wright, James G.
Wright, John.
Wright, John.
Wright, John.
Wright, John.
Wright, Robert.
Wright, Thomas.
Wright, William.
Wright, William.
Wrigley, Joseph.
Wyllie, George.

Wyne, Fred.
Yates, James.
Yeats, James.
Yool, David.
Young, Alan.
Young, David.
Young, George.
Young, John.
Young, Moses.
Young, Richard.
Young, Robert.
Young, Thomas.
Young, William.
Yuill, James.

SINGER HALL

THE Singer Recreation Hall, in which are housed the Roll of Honour and the Memorial to the fallen, presents a very pleasing aspect in which nature combines with the art of the builder. The lawn makes an excellent foreground, and blends with the Welsh green slates which crown the building and the warm tint of the pressed bricks, while the Kilpatrick Hills in the background make the setting one on which it is a pleasure to rest the eye.

The main entrance to the building leads into a spacious entrance hall, from which rises the stairway leading to the galleries of the grand hall. Here the attention is naturally rivetted upon the principal feature, the silent Memorial to the fallen. Impressive in its simple dignity it perpetuates the memory of their sacrifice, and the mighty deeds of the immediate past are recalled and link us with the life of the present. On either side of the entrance hall are cloak rooms and reception rooms, while, in addition, there are on each side of the building a number of other rooms, including reading rooms, recreation rooms and baths.

The grand hall is planned on generous lines, being one hundred and eleven feet long and sixty eight feet broad, while the seating arrangements designed permit of accommodation for upwards of two thousand persons. The roof is an open one, intersected by eight dormar lights, while the colour scheme is laid on delicate tints of green and white which take the full light values. The floor is laid in maple and has been subjected to a special treatment. The stage is fifty feet wide and has been designed to meet the most exacting requirements. The proscenium arch, viewed from the auditorium, suggests spaciousness, and the stage is fitted with the latest appliances for lighting effects and scenery.

To the east of the buildings an excellent bowling green has been laid down, and adjacent to the club house of the bowling green six tennis courts are provided, while football and hockey fields are situated in Boquhanran Road.

In placing this splendidly equipped recreation hall, with its surrounding first-class sports' fields extending to over fifteen acres, at the disposal of their workers, the management of the Company desire to give ample opportunities and facilities for exercise, recreation and rest, recognising that these, with the development of the social virtues, form the basis of all progress.

GRAND HALL   SINGER

INTERIOR OF GRAND HALL, ARRANGED FOR INDOOR SPORTS   SINGER

42

REST AND READING ROOM   SINGER

TENNIS COURTS AND BOWLING GREEN   SINGER

HOCKEY AND FOOTBALL GROUND   SINGER

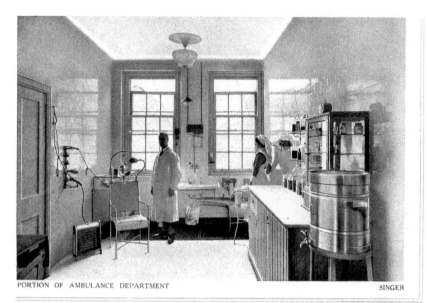

PORTION OF AMBULANCE DEPARTMENT   SINGER

AERIAL VIEW OF FACTORY   SINGER

Printed in the USA
CPSIA information can be obtained
at www.ICGtesting.com
LVHW010423300923
759528LV00010B/1249